I LOVE
HARRY
Are you his ultimate fan?

Buster Books

Contents

About this book

There's no doubt that you're a Directioner. You've followed the boys' journey to superstardom from their humble beginnings on *The X Factor* to world domination!

But the boy that gets your heart fluttering more than all the others is the oh-so-suave Mr Harry Styles.

So, how much do you know about your fave 1D lad? This book is jam-packed with quizzes, puzzles and brain boggling trivia to test your Harry knowledge. There are glossy photos of Harry looking gorgeous for you to gaze at, plus fun fill-in stories and much more.

Get ready to get the lowdown on the curly-haired cutie, and see how much of a super-fan you really are.

It's extraordinHarry!

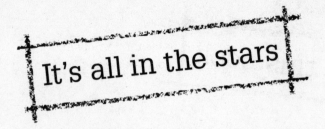

It's all in the stars

DISCOVER WHAT YOUR STAR SIGN SAYS ABOUT YOU, AND FIND OUT HOW YOU COULD FIT INTO HARRY'S LIFE, WITH THE HELP OF THIS HEAVENLY HARRY HOROSCOPE.

⭐ ARIES (21st March – 20th April) ⭐

Ambitious, adventurous and not afraid to take risks, you always see the bigger picture and you're eager to make your mark on the world. You could be Harry's:

Creative director

Your natural confidence and enthusiasm would inspire Harry as you help him to make important decisions about his life in the spotlight.

⭐ TAURUS (21st April – 21st May) ⭐

Everyone needs someone dependable, loyal and strong in their life, and that is what makes you so special – and useful! You have a knack of cutting out the nonsense and getting things done. You could be Harry's:

Personal assistant

Your organizational skills and reliability would make you the ideal person to organize Harry's hectic lifestyle. You'd need to be by his side every step of the way.

GEMINI (22nd May – 21st June)

What a smooth operator you are! You're clever, bubbly and enthusiastic, and great at thinking on your feet. You could be Harry's:

Publicist

Your way with words and wry sense of humour would make sure that even the most hard-headed journalist would fall for Harry's charms.

CANCER (22nd June – 23rd July)

You have a protective, caring and responsible nature and you're brilliant at looking after people. You could be Harry's:

Manager

Your level head means that you can deal with both business and personal matters and make sure that Harry always feels happy about his career and his life.

LEO (24th July – 23rd August)

Confident and outgoing, you like to be the centre of attention, even if Harry is around! So, how best to use your fun but flamboyant nature? Easy! You could be Harry's:

Choreographer

Your infectious sense of fun and excitement would put a spring in Harry's step as you taught him some new moves.

VIRGO (24th August – 23rd September)
You are observant and precise, with a good memory, and you love making things the best they can possibly be. You could be Harry's:

Tour manager
When the 1D boys are away on tour, they experience a roller coaster of emotions and need someone to keep them on track and cheer them up when they feel homesick. If anyone can do it, you can!

 LIBRA (24th September – 23rd October)
Easy-going and diplomatic, you are great at getting along with people and have a reputation as a peace-keeper who can see both sides of an argument. You could be Harry's:

Best friend
Whenever he needs some comfort, good advice, a shoulder to cry on or just to have fun, you'll be there for him.

 SCORPIO (24th October – 22nd November)
You're loyal and generous, a bit of a flirt, and you like to be in control of any situation. You could be Harry's:

Hairstylist
You have a crucial role in maintaining Harry's crowning glory! Harry's locks are adored by Directioners everywhere, so getting them right is of vital importance.

 SAGITTARIUS (23rd November – 21st December)
You welcome change and like to explore new places and make new friends. You're talkative, kind and caring, too. You could be Harry's:

Travel buddy
Making people happy is one of your main aims in life and you'd be sure to make Harry's travel fun and stress free.

★ CAPRICORN (22nd December – 20th January) ★
You're not afraid to shoot for the stars, but you're responsible and patient, too. You could be Harry's:

Business manager
It's your job to handle Harry's money. Buying a house one moment and a car the next, and thinking of the future too – that could be fun!

★ AQUARIUS (21st January – 19th February) ★
Your caring nature makes you want to do something useful for others in your life. It's this unselfish streak that will be perfect in helping Harry to help others. You could be Harry's:

Charity campaigner
Like his mum, Anne, Harry likes to help those in need. Your inventive streak would give Harry some exciting and challenging ways to raise loads of cash for a good cause.

★ PISCES (20th February – 20th March) ★
A sensitive, creative dreamer, you can be a little shy, but you're always loyal and kind. You like to use your brain in an imaginative way. You could be Harry's:

Artistic designer
The 1D stage is a blank canvas just waiting for your talent. With your flair for creativity and wonderful imagination, you would relish the challenge of creating a spectacular backdrop for Harry when he performs.

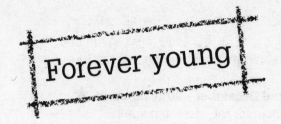

Forever young

HE'S STILL A BIG KID AT HEART   BUT HOW MUCH
DO YOU KNOW ABOUT HARRY'S LIFE BEFORE HE
BECAME FAMOUS? TAKE THIS QUIZ TO FIND OUT, THEN
CHECK YOUR ANSWERS ON **PAGE 91**.

1. What is the name of Harry's drummer pal from his
school band, White Eskimo?
a. Will Swinton
b. Will Sealey
c. Will Sweeny

2. Harry and school pal Will were once told off at a
supermarket for shouting:
a. 'Trolley!'
b. 'Bogeys!'
c. 'Sausages!'

3. What is the name of Harry's sister?
a. Jenny
b. Gemma
c. Janey

4. What was the first song that Harry learned all the words to?

a. 'Girl Of My Best Friend' by Elvis Presley

b. 'Yellow Submarine' by The Beatles

c. 'Honky Tonk Woman' by The Rolling Stones

5. What was the first song that White Eskimo played in their school Battle of the Bands competition?

a. 'Summer Of 69' by Bryan Adams

b. 'School's Out' by Alice Cooper

c. 'Surfin' USA' by The Beach Boys

6. There is a photograph of Harry as a child doing a 'muscle-man' pose and wearing which item of his mum's clothing?

a. Bra

b. Slippers

c. Tights

7. One of Harry's favourite toys as a child was:

a. A train set

b. LEGO

c. An Action Man doll

8. What did Harry say he used to do at school because it made him laugh?

a. Make funny faces

b. Walk like a penguin

c. Moon

9. Harry's first performance, at the age of four, was in a school play as an animal named Barney. What type of animal was he?

a. An owl

b. A dog

c. A mouse

10. According to his mum, Anne, what colours did Harry choose to paint his bedroom at home?

a. Black and white

b. Brown and cream

c. Pink and orange

11. When he was very little, Harry used to be quite creative with his food. What did he used to do?

a. Make snowmen out of mashed potato

b. Arrange the food on his plate so it looked like a face

c. Paint a picture on bread with food colouring, then toast it and eat it

12. What secondary school did Harry attend before he auditioned for *The X Factor*?

a. Holmes Church Comprehensive

b. Holmes Chapel Comprehensive

c. Holmes Manor Comprehensive

Sweet tweets

WE ALL KNOW HARRY'S A REAL 'TWEETHEART' AND HE LIKES TO SHARE HIS LOVE FOR FANS, FAMILY AND FRIENDS VIA THE INTERNET. HERE ARE SOME OF HIS SWEETEST TWEETS.

Work Hard. Play Hard. Be Kind.

....

In such a good mood today:) feel very lucky for the life I have..thank you to all the fans who have put us here. Also..I found my Slippers!!

....

New day....Be nice to people!! :)

....

Rainbows and smiles :)

....

Good morning!! I woke up in a woolly hat...snug.

....

Happy Valentines Day!!! We couldn't do this if it wasn't for you...and we love you for that. Hope everyone has a lovely day! Oui Oui!! .xx

....

Why does everything seem better when it's in a bottle shaped like a bear?

....

Very proud of my mum today, she is on her way home after reaching the top of Mount Kilimanjaro. Thank you to everyone who donated!!

Cringe!

HARRY MIGHT SEEM TO BE EFFORTLESSLY COOL, BUT EVEN HE CAN HAVE EMBARRASSING MOMENTS! READ THESE BLUSH-WORTHY STORIES AND DECIDE WHETHER EACH ONE IS A TRUE CRINGE, OR A FAKE FAIL. YOU CAN CHECK YOUR ANSWERS ON **PAGE 91**.

1. While on a skiing holiday with Louis, Harry was approached by a couple of tourists who pointed a camera at the boys. Assuming they were One Direction fans, Harry and Louis posed with their arms around each other, but they were embarrassed when one of the tourists explained, 'No, we want you to take a photo of *us*.'

☐ True Cringe ☐ Fake Fail

2. During the band's tour of New Zealand, Harry ran down a hotel corridor wearing swimming trunks, a mask and inflatable arm bands, but was left stranded when his One Direction band mates locked him out of his room. Harry hid behind a potted plant until they took pity on him and let him back in!

☐ True Cringe ☐ Fake Fail

3. Harry got a bit carried away while tucking into a bowl of fruit on a photoshoot. He was gobbling down some blueberries when one got stuck in his throat, causing him to choke.

☐ True Cringe ☐ Fake Fail

4. Harry once spent a day wearing a new pair of jeans only to find at the end of the evening that the price sticker was still on the trouser leg.

☐ True Cringe ☐ Fake Fail

5. After a party at JLS singer Marvin Humes's house, a tired Harry curled up and went to sleep in the dog basket!

☐ True Cringe ☐ Fake Fail

6. At Heathrow airport with the boys, Harry playfully pinched Louis's bottom, only to find that it wasn't Louis at all, but a complete stranger!

☐ True Cringe ☐ Fake Fail

7. Harry's most excruciating memory of school is when his mum turned up during a school football match and stopped the game while she made him put on his vest!

☐ True Cringe ☐ Fake Fail

FAIL!

Star date

YOU ENTER A TV COMPETITION TO WIN A DAY WITH
HARRY STYLES HIMSELF ... AND YOU WIN! CREATE THE
DAY OF YOUR DREAMS BY FILLING IN THE GAPS IN THE
STORY BELOW. USE THE IDEAS IN BRACKETS, OR LET
YOUR IMAGINATION RUN RIOT!

On the morning of your big day, a black limo pulls up
outside your house. All the neighbours are watching as
you step out of the front door with a huge smile on your
face. The chauffeur gets out and opens the car door for you
to get into the back seat. Sitting there waiting for you is

Harry. He smiles and hands you a ....

.... (glass of sparkling
orange juice/ bunch of flowers/ box of chocolates)

The limo glides away so smoothly you don't even notice.
You are so excited and nervous that you find you can't
speak, but Harry puts you at your ease by saying,

'..,'

(I'm Harry, pleased to meet you./ You look beautiful!/ This is
going to be fun!)

'So where are we going?' you ask.

Harry smiles. 'It's a secret.'

This is just incredible. You are actually sitting in a limo next to Harry, who is dressed in .... (a white tuxedo with bow tie/ a shirt, blazer and skinny jeans/ a T-shirt, jeans and Beanie) You just wish everyone could see you, but the car windows are tinted so you can only see out. At least it gives you privacy!

Harry leans over and .... (gives you a friendly hug/ gives you a high five/ whispers how much he is looking forward to your day)

'Don't be nervous,' he smiles.

Eventually, the limo pulls up. The chauffeur opens the door to let you both out.

'We're here,' says Harry.

'But where?' you ask.

'I thought you might like to go ....' (to the cinema/ shopping/ ice-skating/ swimming/ for a long walk in the countryside)

You enjoy yourself so much that time absolutely flies by. Then Harry suggests that you go somewhere to eat. And it's your choice. You decide to go

....

(to a swanky restaurant./ for a romantic picnic for two in the park./ to a fast-food outlet so everyone can see you with Harry!)

With lunch over, you wonder what's next on the menu. 'I'm afraid I've got to do a bit of work now,' says Harry. You feel glum. But then he adds, 'I'd like you to come with me. I'm recording a song for our new album. Fancy meeting Louis, Zayn, Niall and Liam?' You are so excited that you can only nod your head like an eager puppy dog!

At the recording studio, Harry introduces you to his One Direction band mates and you watch them perform their new song. You can't wait to you tell your friends!

Then Harry comes over and, to your amazement, asks if you would like to do some backing vocals. You can't believe it – you are actually going to be heard on their new song!

'That was incredible,' says Harry afterwards. Then, to your delight, he adds, '...

....

...............................' (You have such a good voice./ You are great fun./ Louis says you should replace me in One Direction!)

'Is there anything you want to ask me?' says Harry.

You ask him ....
.... (what is the best place he has visited/ what is the most impressive meal he can cook/ what is his best ever Christmas present)

He replies, '..
....'

'It's been a lovely day,' he says. 'Have you enjoyed it?'

'..
.... ,' you reply.

'I'll get the limo to take you home now,' Harry says. You smile, a little sadly. It really has been a great day but all good things must come to an end.

'Well ... you need time to rest and get ready to come out again this evening,' says Harry, with a smile. Then he hands you a golden envelope. You open it and there is an invitation inside. It reads: You are invited to ....
....
.... (One Direction's concert tonight/ a film premiere in the company of Harry and One Direction/ to join Harry for a celebrity-packed party in town)

What a day! And what an evening to look forward to!

Fact-tastic!

OK, SUPER-FAN, IT'S TIME TO PUT YOUR KNOWLEDGE TO THE TEST. READ THE FACTS BELOW AND TICK THE ONES YOU ALREADY KNEW. NO CHEATING! CHECK OUT YOUR SUPER-FAN STATUS USING THE SCORECARD ON **PAGE 22**.

☐ Harry, Liam and Niall were pranked on Nickelodeon when an actress, posing as a TV producer and wearing a fake pregnancy bump, pretended to go into labour just before they were to be interviewed. Louis and Zayn were in on the joke and could barely contain their laughter. Harry really fell for it and was the most anxious of all, calling out, 'Why is no one here? Can somebody help us?'

☐ Harry came up with the name One Direction.

☐ Harry makes a cameo appearance in the video for his friend Ed Sheeran's song 'Drunk', which was filmed backstage at a venue in London.

☐ Nowadays he's certainly a creative guy, but Harry once had a pet hamster who he decided to name … err … Hamster.

☐ He says his worst habit is getting naked all the time!

☐ Each week before he took to the stage during *The X Factor* live shows, poor Harry used to be so nervous that he'd be sick. Thankfully, he's got control of his stagefright now that he's an international superstar.

☐ Harry was embarrassed when Emma Watson heard that he had walked out halfway through a screening of her film, *The Perks of Being a Wallflower*, and tweeted him to ask why.

☐ Harry sometimes suffers with a bad back, and has been advised to take a Pilates class once a week.

☐ All the One Direction boys agree that Harry is the best cook in the band.

☐ Harry was going to learn to play the bass guitar when his first band White Eskimo was formed. He told the other band mates that he couldn't sing.

☐ Harry has bought himself a black Range Rover Sport and an Audi R8 Coupé.

☐ He's a multi-talented lad. As well as his awesome vocal stylings, Harry is a skilled juggler, and he can play the kazoo, too!

☐ Before the boys flew out to Spain for the judges' houses portion of *The X Factor* audition process, they all went to stay in Harry's stepdad's bungalow so they could get to know each other and bond as a group. This proved to be a good strategy, as not only did they blow Simon Cowell away at their audition, they became the best of friends as well. Aww.

SUPER-FAN SCORECARD

Score 0–4
You are a Styles rookie. You've got lots to learn about Harry, but don't worry, this is the sort of studying that's never a chore.

Score 5–9
You are a fabulous fan. Harry's definitely your fave guy, but there's still an air of mystery about him. Get out there and find out as much as you can.

Score 10–13
Wow! You really are a super-fan. Reward yourself for your dedication by watching more 1D videos!

Hot favourites

THINK YOU KNOW HARRY'S FAVE THINGS? TRY THIS FUN
QUIZ TO SEE IF YOU'RE RIGHT ABOUT WHAT MAKES
HARRY SMILE. CHECK YOUR ANSWERS ON **PAGE 91**.

1. What is Harry's top biscuit?
- **a.** Custard cream
- **b.** Hobnob
- **c.** Gingernut

2. Harry thinks what flavour of ice cream is the coolest?
- **a.** Vanilla
- **b.** Pecan
- **c.** Honeycomb

3. His fave comfort food cooked by his mum is:
- **a.** Chicken pie and chips
- **b.** Curry
- **c.** Toad-in-the-hole covered in gravy

4. He was shocked to learn that Niall had never watched
one of his favourite films. Which film was it?
- **a.** *Titanic*
- **b.** *The Lion King*
- **c.** *Finding Nemo*

5. Harry's best joke is:

a. Where do fish get their petrol from? Shell.

b. On which side do chickens have most feathers? On the outside.

c. Why don't ducks tell jokes when they are flying? Because they would quack up.

6. Harry and the other boys are really proud of all the songs on their new album, *Take Me Home*, but which of the tracks is Harry's favourite?

a. 'Live While We're Young'

b. 'Summer Love'

c. 'Heart Attack'

7. What's Harry's favourite topping to put on pancakes?

a. The classic – lemon and sugar

b. Off the wall – banana and chocolate

c. Super sweet – ice cream and sprinkles

8. Which football team does he support?

a. Manchester United

b. Manchester City

c. Barcelona

9. What does Harry say is his guilty pleasure?

a. Watching *Love Actually*

b. Listening to The Spice Girls

c. Reading *Winnie the Pooh*

10. Which restaurant chain would Harry prefer to visit when he is out and about?

   a. McDonald's

   b. KFC

   c. Nando's

11. What is Harry's fave song?

   a. 'Born In The USA' by Bruce Springsteen

   b. 'Flowers In The Window' by Travis

   c. 'Make You Feel My Love' by Adele

12. He's a colourful character, that's for certain, but what is Harry's favourite colour?

   a. Purple

   b. Yellow

   c. Orange

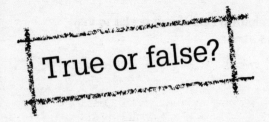

True or false?

READ THE STATEMENTS BELOW AND TICK WHETHER
YOU THINK THEY ARE TRUE OR FALSE. YOU WILL GET
AN EXTRA MARK FOR THE FALSE ANSWERS IF YOU CAN
WRITE DOWN WHICH BAND MEMBER THE STATEMENT IS
REALLY ABOUT. FIND OUT IF YOU'RE RIGHT ON PAGE 92.

1. Harry's hidden talent is a double-jointed thumb.

☐ True   ☐ False. It is ....

2. Harry slipped on stage and fell during a performance
of 'What Makes You Beautiful' at a London club.

☐ True   ☐ False. It was ....

3. Harry terrified his band mates while driving them
around a field in a truck for the video of 'Live While
We're Young'. Part of the truck fell off when he drove
over a bump.

☐ True   ☐ False. It was ....

4. Harry has a habit of dropping his sunglasses down
the toilet!

☐ True   ☐ False. It is ....

5. Harry is claustrophobic and panics when he is in confined spaces.

☐ True ☐ False. It is ....

6. During a US radio interview in Pennsylvania, Harry cheekily held up a poster of Kim Kardashian. On it was a note on which he had scribbled, 'Call me, maybe? ;)'

☐ True ☐ False. It was ....

7. Prankster Louis pulled down Harry's trousers at a service station.

☐ True ☐ False. It was ....'s trousers.

8. A horse once head-butted Harry and it really hurt!

☐ True ☐ False. It was ....

9. As a schoolboy his three best subjects were English, art and drama.

☐ True ☐ False. It was ....

What's your theme song?

Start
It's a sunny day and you want to make the most of it. What do you do?

Call all your friends and have a BBQ in the garden.

It's a fancy dress BBQ, for extra giggles, but what's the theme?

Pop stars. You want to see your friends doing their best diva impressions.

PJs. Super comfortable, relaxed and loads of fun, too.

Head for the beach to soak up some serious rays.

Who do you invite to come with you for some fun in the sun?

Your best friend – you can sunbathe and gossip at the same time.

The new boy in class with the beautiful eyes.

HARRY FOREVER

It's shaping up to be quite a party, but what's on the stereo?

→ 1D, of course. You've got their songs set up on a loop and you're ready to dance.

→ **'Kiss You'**
With your cheeky grin and happy attitude, you're a ray of sunshine. 'Kiss You' matches your joyful personality – you can't help but dance every time you hear it.

→ A playlist of all the coolest new songs, from pop and rock to RnB.

→ **'One Thing'**
You're friendly and fun, with a little bit of mystery about you, too. Everyone who meets you wants to know you better, so 'One Thing' is the song for you.

You spot your crush. How are you going to impress him?

→ Turn on your brightest smile and get ready to wow him.

→ Play it cool. You want him to see your natural beauty.

→ **'Summer Love'**
You love to keep things simple and don't let life stress you out. The laid-back vibe of 'Summer Love' matches your chilled-out personality perfectly.

→ Laze around on the sand, chatting and laughing.

What will you do when you get there?

→ Grab some friends and start a game of beach volleyball.

→ **'Everything About You'**
Whatever you decide to do, people just come running to join in. You've always got a plan up your sleeve for fun, and this song puts a huge smile on your face.

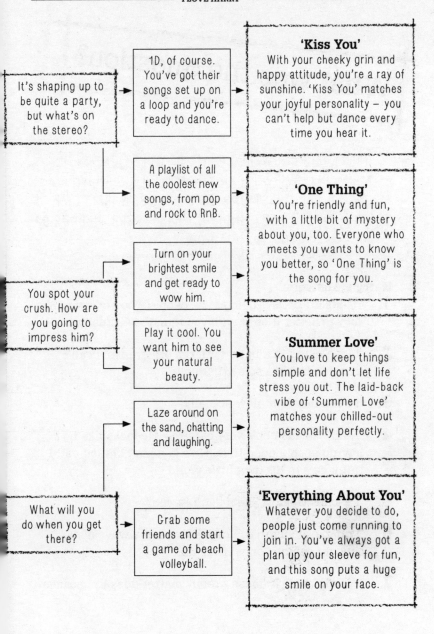

What was the question?

HARRY HAS ANSWERED A LOT OF QUESTIONS IN HIS MANY INTERVIEWS. CAN YOU MATCH HIS ANSWERS BELOW TO THE QUESTIONS OPPOSITE? BEWARE! SOME OF THE QUESTIONS ARE FIENDISHLY FAKE. TURN TO PAGE 92 TO FIND OUT HOW YOU DID.

Harry's Answers:

1. 'There are always going to be people who are acting like they're better friends with you than they actually are.'

2. 'I love being in a band with the other guys. I can't imagine being a solo artist now.'

3. 'I need one right now actually!'

4. 'Niall, because he's very carefree. He looks like he's having such a good time. He's just very chilled out. I think he's in his own little world.'

5. 'Peaches Geldof! She must hate me.'

6. 'I do, but it's hard … I guess you can always make time for things you want to do.'

7. 'Who knows? It doesn't really matter does it, because we are now.'

Questions:

A. Do you really fancy a holiday right now?

B. If you could be one of the other lads for a day, who would it be?

C. Who in One Direction would best be cast as Tarzan?

D. Do you reckon you would have been mates at school?

E. Have you ever had an argument with a celebrity?

F. Do you have time for dating?

G. How many children would you like?

H. Do you ever feel disappointed that you're not a solo artist?

I. How often do you need a hug?

J. We bet all the girls you went to school with have been in touch, haven't they?

K. Have you ever given someone the wrong phone number?

L. Did you think One Direction would be so successful?

Write your answers here:

1. ....

2. ....

3. ....

4. ....

5. ....

6. ....

7. ....

Stole my heart ...

HARRY'S A BIG SOFTIE AT HEART AND OFTEN SHOWS HIS LOVE FOR HIS FAMILY, FRIENDS, FANS AND CHARITABLE CAUSES. READ THE SUPER-CUTE STORIES BELOW, AND RATE THEM ON THE 'CUTE-O-METER' BY SHADING IN THE HEARTS BELOW EACH ONE.

Cute-O-Meter

Aww!

What A Cutie!

Super Sweet!

Cuteness Overload!

I Can't Even Cope With How Cute This Is!

Harry might have a bit of a reputation as a ladies' man, but he's got a heart of gold. 'I like girls but I prefer having a girlfriend,' he says. 'I like having someone I can spoil. Somebody to call up in the middle of the night and just talk to. I like getting close to someone like that.'

One Direction spent a day with seriously ill children at a London hotel, giving big hugs, chatting, taking pics and signing copies of their book as presents. Harry was amazed by the kids' strength. 'They have been through so much, and yet they have such an amazing attitude towards life,' he said.

Seven-year-old Niamh from Leeds was badly burned in an accident at home. 'She spent a long time in hospital, and Harry was her main inspiration to get well,' explained the brave little girl's dad.

The 1D boys are so close, they're like family, and Harry is lucky to be able to count on Zayn and Louis to act as protective older brothers to him when he needs them.

In response to the rumours about Harry and his romances, Zayn remarked, 'He is the baby of the group, but people seem to forget that because of the way that he is and that he is so charming. So it is a little bit upsetting sometimes if you see him with the weight of the world on his shoulders.'

Harry makes no secret of the fact that he sees Coldplay lead singer Chris Martin as a huge inspiration, and it would seem the feeling is mutual. When Harry was at a Coldplay gig, he was stunned when his idol broke into some lyrics from 1D's anthem 'What Makes You Beautiful' to show his appreciation for Harry as a fan.

Harry's mum, Anne, climbed Mount Kilimanjaro for charity, raising money for a cause called Believe In Magic, which supports terminally ill children. Not only did Harry generously sponser his mum £5,000, he encouraged other Directioners to donate to the charity trek on Twitter. His mum raised over £25,000 for the charity, and Harry took to Twitter to tell her how proud he was of her.

Harry's not shy about expressing his love for the other One Direction boys. 'I can't imagine not being with them every day,' he says. 'We're very lucky. The thing I love most about being in this group is that you've always got people around you. If one person is feeling down, you've got four others to cheer them up. That and the fact that after a full day's work, we still choose to hang out together.'

During a concert in Mexico, Harry was singing along with
the boys when he noticed a girl in the front row getting
crushed against the barrier. He bent down to bring it
to the attention of a security guard and then continued
singing. But when the guard was unable to pinpoint the
girl, Harry stopped singing again and pointed her out. He
only continued singing when the girl was lifted to safety.
Then Harry smiled and gave the thumbs up.

Harry and the other 1D boys surprised a group of
special fans by posing as waxworks in famous London
tourist-attraction Madame Tussauds. The fans had been
chosen for this special reward because of the charity work
they do. The five boys kept very still, and came to life at
the last moment, giving the fans the fright of their life, and
a day they'd never forget.

It's no wonder that Harry's mum is one of his biggest fans.
'If I'd had a particularly bad day at work, I'd come home to
find he'd run me a bath and surrounded it with candles and
even cooked me a meal,' she says. 'He just used to usher
me out of the kitchen and say he'd got it all under control.'

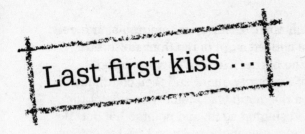

Last first kiss ...

HARRY'S SEEN AS THE FLIRTY ONE IN THE BAND, AND HIS STUNNING SMILE AND OH-SO-CUTE DIMPLES ARE SURE TO MAKE YOU SWOON. HERE ARE HIS THOUGHTS ON LOVE, ROMANCE AND WHAT HE DOES — AND DOESN'T — LOOK FOR IN A GIRL.

Harry enjoys the challenge of winning a girl over. Despite having legions of fans desperate to date him, he's the one that likes to do the chasing:

'The fun part is the chase, so if you speak to me, play a bit hard to get. I think it's attractive when someone turns you down. You don't want someone to say yes straight away, do you?'

He may have a reputation as a Romeo but he insists that most of the girls he is seen with are just friends rather than 'dates':

'I don't want to be viewed as a womanizer or whatever. I know sometimes it might come across in the paper that I'm a bit like that, but I'm really not. I'm not quite as I'm made out to be. I have friends who are girls and sometimes even if I give them a lift home I'm "dating" them.'

He has had his fair share of marriage proposals. The good news is that he loves them. So don't be afraid to ask:

'I don't find the proposals embarrassing at all. I quite like it! I think it's really flattering and quite cute most of the time.'

The modest lad reckons Zayn is the one with the classic good looks in the band:

'I think the most typically good-looking guy is Zayn, with the cheekbones and the jaw.'

He admits that he can be overly-flirtatious but that he is only having fun like any other boy of his age:

'I'm maybe too flirty. But I'm an 18-year-old boy, and I like to have fun. I wouldn't say I'm girl crazy, because that makes me sound like a bit of a womanizer. That isn't really me.'

Barely a day goes by when rumours are not flying around that he is linked with one girl or another. But Harry says that he is very open when he is dating someone and doesn't try to hide it:

'I've never lied about having a girlfriend. I think if you lie, people just want to prove you wrong, so you might as well tell the truth.'

Don't worry if you don't think you are his 'type'. There's a lot more to a girl than looks when it comes to getting his attention:

> 'It's more about the person. How they act, their body language, if they can laugh at themselves. I find ambition really attractive too — if someone's good at something they love doing. I want someone who is driven. And I like a girl who's a bit cheeky, but not too in-your-face.'

He's always being asked what he looks for in a girl, and his fans never tire of hearing his answers. So here's more:

> 'A nice smile, cute, someone who's kind. Someone who is really banterous [a Harry-ism] and puts you down all the time. Someone who's cheeky.'

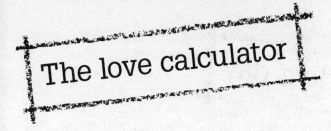

The love calculator

HERE'S A FAST AND FUN WAY TO WORK OUT WHETHER
YOU ARE HARRY'S PERFECT MATCH.

Write your name and his with the word 'LOVES' in the
middle. Then write down how many times the letters L,
O, V, E and S appear in both your names in a line – but
don't include the letters from 'LOVES'. Add together pairs
of numbers – the first and the second, the second and the
third and so on – to work out a final 'percentage'. This tells
you how likely you are to be Harry's dream girl.

Here's an example:

LAUREN TAYLOR  HARRY STYLES

There are three Ls, one O, zero Vs, two Es and two Ss.

Write this as: 3 1 0 2 2

Add together each pair of numbers until you have only
two left.

$$3\ 1\ 0\ 2\ 2$$
$$4\ 1\ 2\ 4$$
$$5\ 3\ 6$$
$$89\%$$

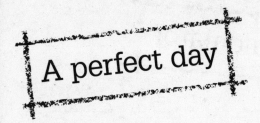

A perfect day

IF YOU COULD GET PAID FOR DAYDREAMING ABOUT HANGING OUT WITH HARRY, YOU'D BE A MILLIONAIRE. HERE ARE THREE PAGES FOR YOU TO DESCRIBE YOUR PERFECT DAY WITH HIM. THE BIG QUESTION IS: WOULD YOU INTRODUCE HIM TO YOUR FRIENDS OR KEEP HIM ALL TO YOURSELF?

Need help getting started?
Try to include the answers to these questions:

- How would your day start?
- How long have you been a fan?
- What do you love most about Harry?
- What are your favourite songs?
- Where would you take him?
- What would he wear?
- What would you eat together?
- What would you say to him?
- What would you want to ask him?
- What would you want him to ask you?
- How would your day end?

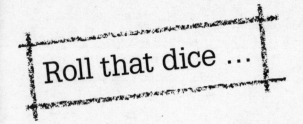

Roll that dice …

TO DISCOVER YOUR DESTINY WITH HARRY, YOU'VE
SIMPLY GOT TO ROLL WITH IT. GRAB A DICE
AND FOLLOW THE INSTRUCTIONS BELOW.

1. Come up with your own ideas for categories **A** to **E**,
and write them in the space for number 6 for each
category.

2. Get rolling! Roll the dice once for each of the
categories. The number you roll is the choice that the
dice has made for you.

3. Write down your future with Harry in the box on the
opposite page, and wait to see if it comes true.

CATEGORIES

A. Where you and Harry will meet:
1. Backstage at a show **2.** At a TV studio **3.** At the airport
4. In a shopping mall **5.** On your street

6. (Your choice) ....

B. What you will do together:
1. Go on a shopping spree **2.** Take dance lessons
3. Sing karaoke **4.** Hit the beach **5.** Stroll through the park

6. (Your choice) ....

C. He will be amazed by your:
1. Eyes **2.** Smile **3.** Banter **4.** Style **5.** Sense of humour

6. (Your choice) ....

D. What he will give you as a gift:
1. A teddy **2.** A heart-shaped necklace **3.** A bunch of
flowers **4.** A love letter **5.** His favourite book

6. (Your choice) ....

E. Where you and Harry will go:
1. Paris **2.** California **3.** India **4.** Florence **5.** Lapland

6. (Your choice) ....

Your future with Harry:

I'm going to meet Harry ....

Together, we will ....

He'll be blown away by my ....

As a present, he will give me ....

We'll travel to ....

Dream date

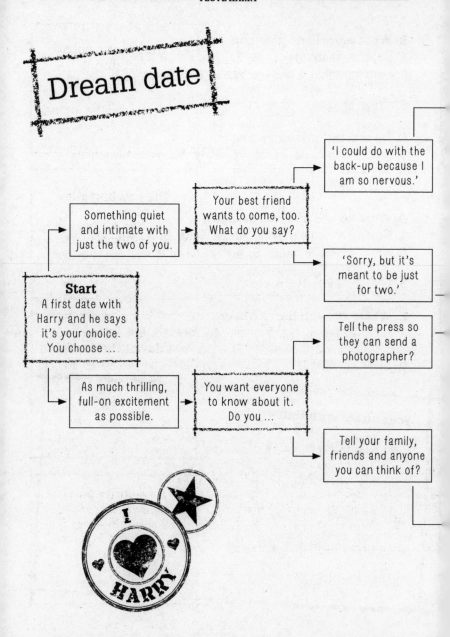

Start
A first date with Harry and he says it's your choice. You choose …

Something quiet and intimate with just the two of you.

Your best friend wants to come, too. What do you say?

'I could do with the back-up because I am so nervous.'

'Sorry, but it's meant to be just for two.'

As much thrilling, full-on excitement as possible.

You want everyone to know about it. Do you …

Tell the press so they can send a photographer?

Tell your family, friends and anyone you can think of?

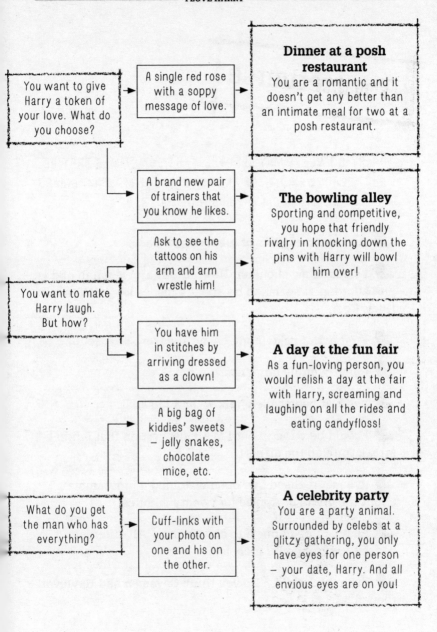

You want to give Harry a token of your love. What do you choose?

A single red rose with a soppy message of love.

Dinner at a posh restaurant
You are a romantic and it doesn't get any better than an intimate meal for two at a posh restaurant.

A brand new pair of trainers that you know he likes.

Ask to see the tattoos on his arm and arm wrestle him!

The bowling alley
Sporting and competitive, you hope that friendly rivalry in knocking down the pins with Harry will bowl him over!

You want to make Harry laugh. But how?

You have him in stitches by arriving dressed as a clown!

A day at the fun fair
As a fun-loving person, you would relish a day at the fair with Harry, screaming and laughing on all the rides and eating candyfloss!

A big bag of kiddies' sweets – jelly snakes, chocolate mice, etc.

What do you get the man who has everything?

Cuff-links with your photo on one and his on the other.

A celebrity party
You are a party animal. Surrounded by celebs at a glitzy gathering, you only have eyes for one person – your date, Harry. And all envious eyes are on you!

HARRY'S TWEETS MAY BE SWEET, BUT SOMETIMES THEY'RE JUST PLAIN WEIRD! HERE ARE SOME OF THE MOST BONKERS BITS FROM THE BRAIN OF MR STYLES.

Avocado ruins lots of great sandwiches.

I slept on my shoulder. Now my left arm is numb and is just hanging. It seems to be about 4 inches longer than my right. Cool.

First carrot cake in my phone speaker...now soup.

I have weirdly large nostrils.

I've just been called 'fellow' and I liked it.

I could be wrong...but I'm almost certain that I didn't streak through the airport.

I've just realised I've been watching a programme about the origin of Apples for twenty minutes.

I have three flannels to choose from. All different consistencies. Spoilt for choice.

Zayn just asked...'Do you think Cavemen had Hayfever' thoughts?

Spot the difference

Can you find eight differences between the top and bottom pictures? You can check your answers on page 92.

A hair-raising adventure

ARE YOU READY TO TAKE CENTRE STAGE IN A HARRY STYLES ADVENTURE? READ THE STORY BELOW AND CHOOSE YOUR OPTIONS CAREFULLY.
WHAT WILL HAPPEN NEXT? YOU DECIDE!

You're at the hairdresser's where you have a Saturday job. While the full-time staff get to be creative in styling and cutting hair, it's your job to prepare and clean up.

You are particularly glum today because it's one of the hairdressers' birthdays, and everyone has gone out to lunch with her to celebrate. Everyone but you, that is. You have to stay behind to look after the salon and to book any appointments. It's sooo boring!

The tinkling bell above the door jolts you from reading about your fave band, One Direction, in a magazine article. They are taking part in a big concert tonight to raise money for children's charities. You'd give anything to go and see the show.

A woman stands in the doorway of the salon looking anxious. 'I desperately need a hairdresser,' she says.

'Certainly,' you reply. 'I'll see when we can fit you in. What about next Tuesday? Or–'

'You don't understand,' the woman interrupts. 'I need one now. And it's not for me. It's for … well, someone quite famous.'

She turns and beckons someone out of a car outside, and in shuffles a figure wearing a hoodie. You can't make out who it is until he pulls the hood off his head. His hair is wet, plastered to his head and covered in slime and weeds. But when he looks up and smiles bashfully, there's no mistaking who it is. It's Harry Styles!

If you decide:

1. To smile back at him and then faint, go to **A**, below.

2. To pretend to be the senior hairstylist, go to **B**, on **page 56.**

A: You find yourself on the floor, gradually regaining consciousness. As your bleary vision clears, you see Harry Styles crouching next to you, looking concerned. His assistant has disappeared.

'Are you okay?' he asks.

'Am I dreaming?' you stammer.

He smiles. 'No, it's really me and I really need your help.'

Harry explains how he was larking around by the river with Louis, Zayn, Liam and Niall when he fell in and got drenched. Worse, his hair became congealed with slime.

With only a few hours to go before tonight's big concert, he needs someone to rescue his hair because his usual hairdresser has fallen sick. Can you fix it?

If you decide:

1. To tell him that you will try your best, go to **A1**, below.

2. To rush out and bring back one of the hairdressers from lunch, go to **A2**, on **page 52**.

A1: Harry sits in the chair, his head back in the sink, as you shampoo away all the river slime. You can't believe that you are actually running your fingers through Harry Styles's hair. It's not easy though. He has a lot of hair and it seems to have soaked up most of the river!

Eventually, you wrap his head in a towel and lead him to another chair, where he sits and looks at himself in the mirror. You have seen how the proper hairdressers perform many times before. You know you can do it. Besides, it's not as if you have to cut anything, right?

'Can you give it a bit of a trim while you're at it?' Harry says suddenly. You feel your tummy performing somersaults but you smile weakly, grab the comb and scissors, and start snipping away.

What do you do?

1. Eek! You get carried away and give him a much shorter style. Go to **A1a**, on **page 53**.

2. You are cautious and style it exactly how it is in the magazines. Go to **A1b** on **page 54**.

A2: Breathless, you arrive back at the salon with Abi, the senior stylist, who looks at Harry and rushes to help. After an expert wash, trim and blow-dry, the smiling face in the mirror is the Harry that you know and love.

He's delighted and gives Abi a big hug. You look a bit disappointed, until he turns and gives you an even *bigger* hug!

'I owe you both, big time,' he says. 'I've got a few hours to spare. Let me treat you. Lunch? Or perhaps we could go to that bowling alley I saw down the road?'

Abi, who knows you are a huge fan of Harry's, gives you a sly wink and tells Harry that she needs to look after the salon. Harry turns to you and smiles. 'Where shall we go?'

If you decide to go:

1. For lunch with Harry, go to **A2a** on **page 54**.

2. To the bowling alley, go to **A2b** on **page 55**.

A1a: You see Harry's face in the mirror. He's not smiling. He looks stunned.

'I … I … I've …' you gasp, but it's no good. You are so nervous that you can't get the words out.

'I know,' says Harry. 'It's shorter than normal.' Then, to your amazement, he turns to you and smiles. 'I like it. In fact … I love it! How can I ever thank you?' he asks.

You're not sure what to say – today's already been better than you'd ever imagined.

Suddenly, Harry snaps his fingers. 'The other boys are at the hotel, do you want to come and hang out with us? I think we're gonna order some pizza and chill out before the show …'

OMG! You can't keep the smile from your face, and you throw your arms around Harry, who bursts out laughing.

You spend the rest of the day chatting to all five of the boys, taking pics together and having a real laugh.

Just when you think things couldn't get any better, the boys give you a VIP pass to that evening's concert, and they open the show by thanking Harry's favourite new stylist – you!

THE END

A1b: Harry grins as you show him his cut. 'You've saved the day,' he says. 'I have a couple of hours to spare – fancy showing me round the town?'

You stroll through the town centre with Harry, chatting and laughing. Suddenly, he is spotted by a large crowd of One Direction fans, who surge towards him. Harry ducks down an alleyway and he calls for you to follow him, but there are so many fans around by now that you lose sight of him. Later, one of them tells you that he got into his car and drove off. You walk sadly home, wishing you'd had more time to spend with Harry.

When you get home, you hear a whistle from across the street. You turn to see a black limo parked opposite your house. Looking at you through the open window is Harry, with a broad smile on his face.

'I was hoping I would find you,' he says. 'I didn't get the chance to say goodbye. Hop in – we've got a gig to go to!'

THE END

A2a: Harry takes you to the swankiest restaurant in town. You both tuck in to a delicious meal, but suddenly his face turns pale as he spots a huge crowd gathering outside. Uh oh – you've been spotted!

His assistant pops her head round the door and whispers, urgently, 'I'll stall them, Harry, but you two will have to find another exit.'

You find the chef and ask him where the back exit goes to.

You realize that you know a network of alleys behind the restaurant leading to your own home.

Quickly, you scribble on a scrap of paper. 'Give your assistant this address,' you tell Harry. 'Then follow me.'

You sneak through the back, then run through the alleyways together, laughing and breathless. When you arrive in your street, Harry's car is already waiting but the evening isn't over yet. Harry tells you he can wait for ten minutes if you want to change out of your work clothes – he's taking you to the big gig as his guest!

THE END

A2b: Outside the salon, a black stretch limo is waiting, and the gentlemanly singer holds the door open for you as you clamber in.

The car is AMAZING, with built-in computer games, a fridge for drinks and snacks, and a wide-screen TV.

'Help yourself,' says Harry. He flips up a section of the seat and reveals dishes of crisps, pizza slices, cakes and chocolate treats.

Arriving at the bowling alley, you are in for another surprise – all four of Harry's band mates have come along to play. You're so excited that you barely knock down a single pin during the game, but it doesn't matter, because you're spending the day with One Direction!

THE END

B: Harry settles into the chair. As you shampoo his hair, you are in such a daydream that you don't notice the crowds of fans gathering outside the salon, chanting Harry's name.

Just then, disaster strikes. Muscling her way through the crowd outside is Abi, the chief stylist, and she looks angry. Your cover is about to be blown and there's nowhere to run.

'I think I'd better lock the door,' you say, thinking quickly. 'Some of the fans might try to come in.'

You attempt to ignore the furious look on Abi's face as she tries to open the door, then begins to bang loudly on the glass and call your name.

Turning up the radio to drown out the noise, you know you can't get away with it much longer and cutting Harry's hair under this sort of pressure could be disastrous.

If you decide to:

1. Set off the fire alarm and escape out of the back door with Harry, go to **B1**, below.

2. Let Abi in and confess, go to **B2**, on **page 57**.

B1: The clang of the fire alarm makes Harry jump.

'Oh no!' he says. 'What are we going to do? I can't go out the front, there are too many people.'

'This way,' you say, confidently. You open the fire exit and Harry, hair dripping wet, hesitates.

'You go first,' he begs. 'Check the coast is clear.'

You pop into the smelly, litter-strewn alleyway behind the shop and gesture to Harry to follow. It really stinks, but Harry laughs at the scrunched up look on your anxious face.

'All part of the job,' he says with a smile. 'In a minute, I think my car will find us.'

As he speaks, a black limo pulls up at the end of the alley and Harry gestures you to jump in. 'Come on,' he says. 'You can finish my hair back at the hotel.'

If you decide to:

1. Jump in and carry on pretending you're the stylist, go to **B1a** on **page 58**.

2. Tell Harry the truth, go to **B1b** on **page 59**.

B2: 'What do you think you're doing?' yells Abi, as you open the door and finally let her in. 'You're not supposed to take any clients while we're at lunch.'

Harry looks over, shocked and confused, and Abi stops in her tracks.

'You're ... you're ...' she stumbles.

'Yes, I am,' laughs Harry, 'and your friend was just trying to help a boy in need. Has she done anything wrong?'

'Yes, I have,' you chime in, 'I lied. I said I was the senior stylist and I am really only the assistant. I just wanted to help you.'

'Thanks for trying to help me out,' says Harry. 'It means a lot. But who is going to sort my hair?'

If you decide to:

1. Duck out and let Abi take over, go to **B2a**, on **page 60**.

2. Tell Abi that you'd like to go ahead and try the style you had in mind, go to **B2b** on **page 61**.

B1a: You hand Harry a towel that you managed to grab as you rushed out of the salon and he smiles. 'What now?'

'Erm ...' you stutter, not sure how to continue.

'I know you are not the senior stylist because the badge on your white coat says "Junior assistant". I don't care! You were willing to help out and that's good enough for me. Now, how are you with a hairdryer?'

You flush with shame, but you're soon laughing along with the 1D singer. 'Not bad, as it happens,' you giggle, 'and that really is the truth.'

Back at Harry's hotel, as you style his famous locks, Harry asks about your dream of being a top stylist one day and listens as you talk about opening your own salon. When you've finished, he looks in the mirror and smiles. 'You will be head and shoulders above the rest when you do,' he says. 'I'll be your first client.'

THE END

B1b: 'You mean you aren't a stylist at all?' says Harry, with a shocked look on his face.

'Well,' you stammer, 'I'm really just an assistant. Sorry, Harry, I just didn't want to let you down.'

The star smiles and gestures for you to come with him anyway. 'I need someone to make me look good for tonight's show, so why not give it a go?'

To your amazement, the result is pretty good, and Harry thinks so, too. Before he heads out to the show, he gives you a hug and presses something into your hand – it's two tickets to the show, plus a backstage pass!

That night, you and your BFF have the best seats in the house. You feel a special glow of pride when Harry walks on stage with his hair looking immaculate, and the crowd goes WILD.

THE END

B2a: Abi's face softens as she realizes that you did what anybody else would have done when their idol turned up asking for help.

'I understand,' she says. 'I'll take it from here.'

You are feeling a bit upset that you can't finish the job, when Harry pipes up again.

'But you've been so good to me, how about you and I hang out this afternoon and I introduce you to the boys? Abi, you can come, too.'

'Thanks, but I can't leave the salon,' says Abi, with a wink. 'You can take the rest of the afternoon off, though, you've earned it.'

Harry offers you his arm and walks you to a sleek, black limo. You get in, and the car pulls up outside a theme park.

'The park is closed to the public for the afternoon,' says Harry. 'They invited us along to test out some rides. I thought you might like to join us all.'

Inside the park, you can hardly contain your excitement as Harry introduces you to Liam, Zayn, Niall and Louis. What a roller coaster of a day!

THE END

B2b: 'Well,' Abi says, 'as his number one fan, you know Harry's style better than most people. If it's okay with him, I'm happy for you to have a go.'

'Fine by me,' laughs Harry.

Excited, you grab the gel and the brushes and off you go, creating the most important masterpiece of your life.

Harry looks in the mirror and grins. 'Wow!' he says. 'It's never looked better. I owe you a BIG thank you, and I have just the thing.'

Harry takes you through the crowd of excited fans outside and into a waiting car, which speeds off.

Next stop is a designer store, where Harry has made sure you have the place to yourself as you pick out a dress.

Finding one you love, you gasp at the price tag, but Harry smiles. 'You deserve it, for trying to help me out and risking your job in the process.'

'But what will I wear it to?' you ask.

'Tonight's show, of course,' he says. 'You're our VIP guest.'

THE END

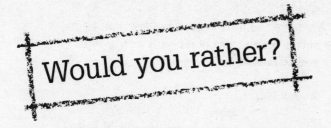

Would you rather?

WHAT WOULD YOU DO IF YOU HAD THE CHANCE TO
SPEND SOME TIME WITH HARRY? READ THE FOLLOWING
ALTERNATIVES AND MARK YOUR CHOICE FOR EACH ONE.
FOR EVEN MORE FUN, YOU MIGHT LIKE TO COMPARE
YOUR ANSWERS WITH THOSE OF YOUR FRIENDS.

Would you rather ...

Be Harry's hairstylist? ⟷ Be his clothes stylist?

Watch him and
One Direction record ⟷ Watch him at a magazine
their latest song? photoshoot?

Go on holiday with him? ⟷ Do backing vocals for a
One Direction song?

Go to a swanky ⟷ Go shopping with him?
restaurant with him?

Be invited to meet his ⟷ Take him home to meet
family at home? your family?

Go to the cinema together? ⟷ Watch a DVD at his house?

Help him write a new song? ⟷ Appear in a One Direction music video?

Go surfing with him? ⟷ Invite him to spend a day at your school?

Design a sizzling stage outfit for him? ⟷ Help him with some dance moves?

Go to the zoo? ⟷ Go ice-skating?

Go for a walk in the countryside? ⟷ Go sightseeing in town?

Have him sing you a romantic song? ⟷ Have him tell you his funniest jokes?

Take a ride together in a gondola in Venice? ⟷ Go skydiving together?

All directions!

UP, DOWN, FORWARDS, BACKWARDS, EVEN DIAGONALLY — YOU NEED TO SEARCH EVERY WHICH WAY IN THIS PUZZLE TO FIND PEOPLE, PLACES AND SONGS THAT MEAN A LOT TO HARRY. TURN TO **PAGE 93** IF YOU GET STUCK!

TAKE ME HOME

THE BEATLES

CHRIS MARTIN

ELVIS PRESLEY

GEMMA

UP ALL NIGHT

CHESHIRE

'LITTLE THINGS'

ONE DIRECTION

EDWARD

Y	C	J	E	P	M	R	J	A	T	T	P	S	T	W
E	R	H	M	R	X	Q	M	M	H	A	G	O	A	G
L	G	F	R	U	I	M	M	E	X	N	I	O	K	D
S	M	E	F	I	E	H	B	O	I	E	L	Q	E	T
E	H	F	L	G	S	E	S	H	O	T	T	K	M	Z
R	Q	T	L	B	A	M	T	E	H	O	J	D	E	S
P	D	Q	J	T	B	E	A	J	H	R	L	R	H	Q
S	K	J	L	D	L	K	W	R	Z	C	P	A	O	L
I	R	E	T	T	U	J	M	W	T	D	P	W	M	G
V	S	K	T	D	D	G	S	L	P	I	B	D	E	C
L	L	I	N	E	D	I	R	E	C	T	N	E	N	Z
E	L	D	T	J	G	T	E	D	E	N	M	A	O	I
T	H	G	I	N	L	L	A	P	U	I	Z	T	K	D
O	J	T	V	R	U	N	O	I	F	F	W	U	J	S
R	N	O	N	E	D	I	R	E	C	T	I	O	N	V

True-fan timeline

HARRY HAS HAD A METEORIC RISE TO STARDOM AND
HIS FANS HAVE BEEN WITH HIM EVERY STEP OF THE
WAY. WE'VE LISTED SOME MAJOR MOMENTS IN HIS LIFE
BUT SOME DETAILS ARE MISSING. FILL IN THE SPACES
WITH THE WORDS AND DATES ON **PAGE 69**. CHECK YOUR
ANSWERS ON **PAGE 94**.

....(1): Harry Styles is born in
Holmes Chapel, Cheshire. At school, he and some friends
form a band called White Eskimo. Harry is the lead singer.

June 2010: At his first audition for *The X Factor* Harry sings

....(2) by Stevie Wonder.

July 2010: Harry doesn't make it through to the Boys
category and says he's 'gutted'.

September 2010: After Simon Cowell forms One Direction
from individual solo singers, they perform at his house in
LA, singing Natalie Imbruglia's 'Torn'.

October 2010: In the first of the live shows, One Direction
sing Coldplay's 'Viva La Vida' to much acclaim.

December 2010: One Direction perform with Robbie Williams during *The X Factor* live final. Harry describes singing with Robbie as 'an honour'. They come third in the competition, losing out to winner Matt Cardle and runner-up Rebecca Ferguson. 'Of course we're disappointed,' says Harry.

March 2011: Harry proudly poses with the rest of the band as they release their first book, *One Direction: Forever Young*, which climbs to the top of the bestseller list.

August 2011: Harry arrives at the Radio 1 London studios with his band mates for the first play of One Direction's debut single 'What Makes You Beautiful'.

September 2011: Their debut single reaches No 1 on the UK Top 40. It goes on to spend 19 consecutive weeks in the charts.

September 2011: Harry first reveals he has a crush on *The Xtra Factor* presenter Caroline Flack when he gets a friend to tweet her.

February 2012: He flies to the US with One Direction to begin a Stateside tour.

February 2012: 1D win ....(3) at the Brit Awards. The boys beat nine other acts to scoop the prize for their debut track 'What Makes You Beautiful'.

March 2012: One Direction become the first British group to go straight to No 1 on the US Billboard 200 chart with their album *Up All Night*.

...............................(4): One Direction arrive in Sydney for their mini-tour of Australia and New Zealand.

May 2012: 'What Makes You Beautiful' goes double platinum in the US. The boys celebrate being one of the most successful British boy bands to make it in America.

August 2012: On a moving carnival float, the One Direction boys perform 'What Makes You Beautiful' at the amazing

....(5) in London.

August 2012: One Direction announce that their second album will be called *Take Me Home*.

The record's lead single 'Live While We're Young' becomes the fastest selling pre-ordered song in history.

September 2012: One Direction win three MTV Video Music Awards in Los Angeles. They beat the likes of

....(6) and Rihanna in the Best Pop Video category for 'What Makes You Beautiful' and also collect Best New Artist. The distinctive awards are astronaut figures and, taking the stage to collect the second one, Harry says, 'To win one Moonman is amazing. To win two is incredible and to perform is absolutely ridiculous, so thank you so much for having us.' After belting out 'One Thing', they pick up their third award for Most Share-Worthy Video.

November 2012: They release their second album *Take Me Home*.

November 2012: They achieve a UK chart double with their new single, 'Little Things', reaching No 1 and their album, *Take Me Home*, doing the same.

November 2012: One Direction perform 'Little Things' before the Queen at *The Royal Variety Performance*. Harry was nervous about being introduced to the Queen. He described comedian Ronnie Corbett, who also appeared on the show, as 'a legend'.

February 2013: One Direction embark on a world tour.

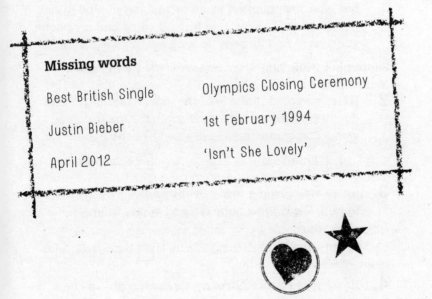

Missing words

Best British Single

Olympics Closing Ceremony

Justin Bieber

1st February 1994

April 2012

'Isn't She Lovely'

Super-fans

HARRY IS SURE THAT DIRECTIONERS ARE THE BEST FANS
IN THE WORLD BUT SOMETIMES THINGS CAN GET A BIT
OVER THE TOP. TRY TO WORK OUT WHICH OF THESE FAN
FACTS ARE TRUE AND WHICH ARE FALSE. CHECK YOUR
ANSWERS ON **PAGE 94**.

1. A fan dropped her mobile phone into Harry's pocket
but was disappointed when he instantly found it and
gave it back. The girl told him, 'If you'd had my phone,
you'd have had to meet up with me to give it back.'

☐ True Tale   ☐ Fan Fake

2. Harry revealed that one of the most imaginative and
downright bizarre gifts ever given to One Direction
was a box of mushrooms dressed like the band!

☐ True Tale   ☐ Fan Fake

3. Harry was given a teddy bear by a fan who explained
to him, 'Teddy is a huge fan and wants to live
with you.'

☐ True Tale   ☐ Fan Fake

4. Harry was knocked over by screaming girls as he
got out of a car at a studio in central London. He was

helped up and managed to compose himself and smile at the fans as he made his way into the safety of the building.

☐ True Tale   ☐ Fan Fake

5. An excited fan was determined to get Harry's attention as he and the boys emerged from a radio studio in Ireland. Despite being held back amongst a crowd behind barriers, she took aim and let fly with a bag of sweets, hitting Harry and causing him to double up with pain. Whoops!

☐ True Tale   ☐ Fan Fake

6. Security guards struggled to hold back a Directioner who said she needed to get into Harry's hotel room because it was her first day as his new assistant hairstylist and she was panicking because she was late for her appointment.

☐ True Tale   ☐ Fan Fake

7. Harry was impressed when five fans approached the band in Boston, USA, each dressed as one of the One Direction boys.

☐ True Tale   ☐ Fan Fake

8. One enterprising group of 'mobile' fans follows One Direction around on skateboards. Harry couldn't believe his eyes when he first saw them.

☐ True Tale   ☐ Fan Fake

9. Emerging from a TV studio in Manchester, Harry shook hands with some of the fans outside but was surprised to see one of them holding a toy doll of him on which she had painted a beard. When he asked her why, she explained that she liked men with beards!

☐ True Tale   ☐ Fan Fake

10. A misguided fan keeps giving Harry olives as presents. The only problem is that Harry hates olives!

☐ True Tale   ☐ Fan Fake

11. When fans were outside his family home in Cheshire, Harry's best mate from school, Will, arrived in his car. Harry sneaked out of the back entrance and ducked down inside the car, while Will threw some coats over him. The suspicious fans peered through the car windows. Harry whispered to Will to let him know when they had gone and, for a joke, Will gave him the all clear. But as Harry whipped the coats off, he was greeted by screaming fans.

☐ True Tale   ☐ Fan Fake

12. A girl in Singapore handed Harry an impressive-looking white and gold invitation. When he opened it, he was startled to see that it was an invite to his own wedding! She was the bride and he was the groom.

☐ True Tale   ☐ Fan Fake

Inside story

YOU ARE A TOP JOURNALIST AND HAVE FINALLY
MANAGED TO GET AN HOUR'S INTERVIEW WITH HARRY IN
HIS HOTEL ROOM. IMAGINE THE SCENE, YOUR QUESTIONS
AND HIS ANSWERS, AND FILL IN THE BLANKS BELOW.

You arrive at the hotel and see a crowd of One Direction
fans outside. Making your way through them, you are
stopped by a security guard outside. But after showing him
your press card, you are allowed through.

In the hotel's reception, you are greeted by Harry's
publicist, and you both get into a lift that takes you to the
top floor. Walking along the carpeted hallway, the publicist
stops and knocks on a door. It is opened by another
assistant, who ushers you inside. There, sitting on a large
sofa, is Harry Styles.

After shaking his hand, you sit down on a chair opposite
him and prepare to begin.

'Harry, I know you get asked a lot of questions, and I've
been trying to think of one that you have never been asked

before. And I came up with this: ....

.... ?'

Harry smiles and says: '...'

Then he thinks about the question and answers: '................
....'

You are pleased with his honest answer, and it gives you
confidence. You tell him that you are going to throw a
series of oddball questions at him. Harry grins and says:

'
....'

'Have you ever had a supernatural experience?' you ask.
'Ghosts, aliens or anything unexplainable?'

To your surprise, he immediately says, '................................
....'

On a roll now, you ask, 'If there was a fire in your house,
what would be the first thing you grabbed as you
rushed out?'

Harry replies: '..
....
....'

'Okay,' you say. 'What was the best birthday present you
ever had?'

Harry wastes no time in answering: '....................................
....,'

'And the worst?'

He says: '..,'

You ask Harry if he is enjoying this interview.

He laughs and says: '...,'

Determined to keep the interview original and fresh you ask:

'...,'

And he replies: '...,'

Then you get cheeky and he starts to blush a little when you ask him your most personal question so far: '..................

....,'

But, taking a deep breath, he answers, '..................................

....,'

Wow! This is going to be some read. In fact, it could turn out to be the best interview he has ever done. You can see the headlines now: ....

..............................., or perhaps ....

....

The publicist brings in a tray of biscuits and cakes.

'Oh yeah!' remarks Harry, reaching for the tray.

'..................................... are my favourite biscuits. What are yours?'

You tell him: '...'

To your surprise, he turns the tables on you and starts asking you questions! 'So, have you ever had a supernatural experience?'

You laugh and reply: '...
....'

Then he asks which is your favourite One Direction song.

You don't hesitate in telling him: '.......................................'

But, keen to focus back on him, you offer him another biscuit and then say, 'Talking of food ... I've heard you enjoy cooking. What meal would you be able to impress me with?'

Harry replies with a twinkle in his gorgeous eye: '................
....'

The publicist comes over to tell you that it is time to end the interview. You get up and shake hands with Harry. He surprises you asking: '...
....
....'

Now to write up your dream interview with Harry.

EXCLUSIVE INTERVIEW WITH HARRY

by _____ (write your name)

_____

_____

_____

_____

_____

_____

_____

_____

_____

_____

_____

_____

_____

_____

_____

_____

_____

_____

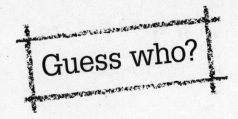

Guess who?

READ THE QUOTES FROM HARRY BELOW AND SEE IF YOU CAN WORK OUT WHO OR WHAT HE IS TALKING ABOUT. YOU CAN FIND THE ANSWERS ON **PAGES 94–95** TO SEE IF YOU'VE CRACKED THE CLUES.

1. 'Yes, I think I would actually. I'd have to raise a lot of money, but if I raised enough money I would.'

Clue: Even if it was for a good cause, you'd cry if Harry lost his crowning glory.

What is it? ....

2. 'I'd keep laughing and stuff in court, it'd be awful.'

Clue: This could have been Harry's career if he wasn't in One Direction.

What is it? ....

3. 'You never think that you'd have yourself in, like, little form.'

Clue: This is one version of Harry that you could take home.

What is it? ....

4. 'She'll do it and make it all amazing and then I'll move it around, so she hates me!'

Clue: It's gotta be a tough job keeping Mr Styles styled!

Who is it? ....

5. 'He's just pretty isn't he? Just look at him! His cheekbones!'

Clue: If Harry was a girl, he'd want to know 'vas happenin'' with this gorgeous lad!

Who is it? ....

6. 'He is such a great singer, performer and writer. If I could be as talented as any musician, it would be him all day long.'

Clue: Harry's musical idol won't be causing 'Trouble'. He might take you to 'Paradise', where the sun is bright 'Yellow' and try to 'Fix You'.

Who is it? ....

7. 'He's a genuine, kind-hearted boy ... Someone being genuine is really important to me. I think if you were his girlfriend, he would treat you really well.'

Clue: Awww. There's a real bromance going on here, and Harry thinks this guy would never cause you Payne ...

Who is it? ....

So Styles-ish

HARRY HAS STYLE ALRIGHT, AND HE ISN'T AFRAID TO EXPERIMENT. ONE DIRECTION STYLIST CAROLINE WATSON SAYS, 'HARRY'S LOOK IS PREPSTER MEETS ENGLISH SCHOOLBOY.' STUDY THE STYLE-O-METER AND RATE HARRY'S STYLE STATEMENTS BY FILLING IN THE STARS UNDER EACH DESCRIPTION.

Style-O-Meter

★☆☆☆☆ Mmmm ...

★★☆☆☆ Semi-Stylish

★★★☆☆ Super Slick

★★★★☆ Hot Or What?

★★★★★ Boy, That's *Sizzling* Style(s)!

Mr Bean

He loves a woolly Beanie hat – especially in the winter.
Pulled down low over his ears it certainly gives him the
snuggly, cute factor. But quite how he manages to get it
over his curly mop is a mystery.

Blaze of glory

He's put the blazer back in fashion. Harry has a seemingly
never-ending wardrobe of colourful blazers ... grey, brown,
tweed, red velvet, blue velvet ... Often worn with the
sleeves rolled up to show a funky lining, worn over a simple
T-shirt or plain shirt.

The DJ

There's nothing mean and menacing about Harry in a
dinner jacket. This is no James Bond look with a hint of
danger. The cheeky lad loves a bow-tie and complements it
with a huge smile. It's a clean and polished look that even
your mum would like.

Skinny leg

He loves skinny jeans of all colours — brown, beige, purple — you name it. It gives him a fun, casual look — especially combined with Converse footwear.

T-time

His T-shirt collection is enormous. Round-neck or V-neck, he doesn't mind. Harry has a variety of colours but he has a particular fondness for simple, plain white, which gives him a fresh, cool look — as if he has just stepped out of a washing powder advert!

Suits you

Ultra tight and shiny, his suits are so sharp you could cut your hand on them. Worn over a formal shirt with a thin tie or even a bow-tie, open-necked or with a casual T-shirt, Harry looks dapper and he knows it!

Tattoo much

Harry got his first tattoo when he was 18 — a star on the inside of his left arm. Now he can't seem to stop! Amongst his body art is a line from a song by The Temper Trap, 'Sweet Disposition', which reads: 'won't stop till we surrender'. He has a tiny 'A' in the crook of his elbow, an iced gem biscuit, comedy and tragedy drama masks, the initials S.M.C.L. and two birds on his chest.

Hair we go

His hair is a major part of his image, but Harry likes to play it down – even if it won't stay down! 'I don't do anything to it, really,' he says. 'It's kind of like, out of bed and then dry it. I think I might go bald soon. I'm worried that it will all just fall out.'

But One Direction hairstylist Lou Teasdale lets us in on a little secret. 'Harry has fine hair, so I use dry shampoo to stop it from looking flat.'

Dream big

HARRY'S DREAMS HAVE LED HIM FROM A SCHOOL BAND TO INTERNATIONAL STARDOM WITH ONE DIRECTION, BUT HE HAS NOT LET STARDOM GO TO HIS CURLY HEAD. READ WHAT HE HAS TO SAY BELOW, THEN ADD YOUR OWN THOUGHTS AND ASPIRATIONS.

'Singing's what I want to do, and if people who can make that happen for me don't think that I should be doing that, then it's a major setback in my plans.'

What is your plan or ambition in life?

....

....

If you were to enter *The X Factor*, what song would you sing?

....

'There's a lot of pressure to be a good role model.'

How is Harry a good role model to young people?

....

....

What are the disadvantages of becoming a celebrity?

....

‘We're just five normal teenager lads who have been having a lot of fun, working very hard. We've been very lucky.’

Why do you think some people are successful and others are not?

....

If you were to form a five-piece group with your friends, which ones would you choose?

....

....

‘I think it's good that you don't have a moment where you think "I've made it" because it's important to keep changing your goals.’

Which achievement in your life are you most proud of?

....

How would you like to develop it further to the next stage?

....

....

'Our fans are amazing. We really wouldn't be able to do this without them.'

Harry is very appreciative of his fans. Who have you been a fan of in your lifetime?

....

What is the most 'fan-like' thing you have ever done?

....

'Not many people get this opportunity. Our lives are amazing and we're very grateful.'

Describe a time when you have seized an opportunity and made the most of it.

....

Why do you think that Harry is grateful?

....

'We just want to work hard, have fun and see what happens.'

Describe a time when you have worked really hard for something and got it.

....

....

Have you ever thought something would be difficult or boring and it's turned out to be fun and a good thing after all? What was it?

....

'We all keep each other grounded and we have a good team around us. And our families are very supportive and are good at keeping us grounded.'

When have your parents, family or friends given you support when you have most needed it?

....

When did you give a friend or family member support in their time of need?

....

'You must never say, "You've done it." You need to make sure you are always on your toes. Trying to be better. To make sure you don't become complacent.'

Who has given you the most encouragement in life?

....

What is the best advice that you have ever been given?

....
....

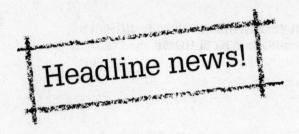

Headline news!

THE WORLD'S MEDIA CAN'T GET ENOUGH OF NEWS ABOUT HARRY BUT SOME HARRY HEADLINES ARE POSITIVELY EYE-POPPING ... HAVE A LOOK AT THE HEADLINES BELOW. SOME ARE REAL. SOME ARE MADE UP. CAN YOU SPOT WHICH ONES HAVEN'T (YET!) APPEARED IN THE PRESS? THE ANSWERS ARE ON **PAGE 95**.

'I HAVE 7000 GIRLFRIENDS'
We know there is no shortage of girls willing to be his latest date but is he really going out with 7000 different ones?

☐ True News   ☐ Fake Fail

'HARRY STYLES TOO PRETTY TO PLAY FOOTBALL'
Despite wanting to play football in the US for a celebrity team, his management have refused to let him in case he gets injured, because he's too handsome!

☐ True News   ☐ Fake Fail

'HAIRY SPIDER SPIED ON HARRY'
A friend played a trick on him during a school camping trip by hanging a hairy toy spider above his sleeping bag. When Harry woke and saw it, he screamed ... loudly!

☐ True News   ☐ Fake Fail

'HARRY STYLES WILL BE UP ALL NIGHT IN SPOOKY NEW HOME'

According to this story, Harry bought a home which is haunted by legendary highwayman Dick Turpin. Not only has his ghost been seen, but the sound of his horse, Black Bess, can be heard outside.

☐ True News   ☐ Fake Fail

'I'M A BIG KNIT!'

To pass away the time on tour, he has taken to knitting – much to the amusement of his band mates. It is a skill he was taught by his mum.

☐ True News   ☐ Fake Fail

'HARRY STYLES HANGS OUT WITH JAMES CORDEN. START OF A NEW CELEBRITY BROMANCE?'

It seems Harry wants to be BFFs with James Corden.

☐ True News   ☐ Fake Fail

'HARRY'S CLOSE ENCOUNTER'

A spooky account of him seeing a flying saucer in the skies above his home when he was a child.

☐ True News   ☐ Fake Fail

'HARRY GETS LIPPY'

Apparently, the poor boy's lips suffer in the cold so much that he is launching his own brand of lip balm.

☐ True News   ☐ Fake Fail

SO HARRY'S YOUR NUMBER ONE HUNK — USE THIS SPACE
TO WRITE DOWN YOUR TOP TEN FAVOURITE THINGS
ABOUT THE STYLES-ISH ONE. HOW WILL YOU LIMIT IT
TO ONLY TEN?

1.

2.

3.

4.

5.

6.

7.

8.

9.

10.

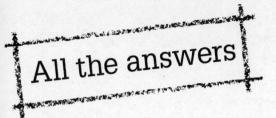

All the answers

Forever young
Pages 10–12

1.	c	**4.**	a	**7.**	b	**10.**	b
2.	b	**5.**	a	**8.**	c	**11.**	c
3.	b	**6.**	a	**9.**	c	**12.**	b

Cringe!
Pages 14–15

1.	True Cringe	**5.**	True Cringe
2.	Fake Fail	**6.**	True Cringe
3.	True Cringe	**7.**	Fake Fail
4.	True Cringe	**8.**	Fake Fail

Hot favourites
Pages 23–25

1.	b	**7.**	c
2.	c	**8.**	a
3.	c	**9.**	a
4.	a	**10.**	a
5.	b	**11.**	c
6.	a	**12.**	b

True or false?
Pages 26–27

1. False – It is Zayn.
2. True
3. False – It is Louis.
4. True
5. False – It is Niall.
6. True
7. False – It was Niall's trousers.
8. True
9. False – It was Zayn.

What was the question?
Pages 30–31

1. J
2. H
3. I
4. B
5. K
6. F
7. D

Spot the difference
In picture section

1. Louis's last button is missing.
2. Liam now has two wristbands.
3. Liam's watch has changed colour.
4. Liam's trophy base has changed colour.
5. Harry is missing a necklace.
6. Harry's flower has changed colour.
7. Zayn has a long sleeve.
8. Niall's missing a wristband.

All directions!
Pages 64–65

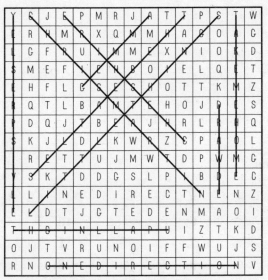

As every super-fan knows, EDWARD is Harry's middle name, GEMMA is his sister's name, and CHRIS MARTIN of Coldplay is a musician he really admires. Harry was born in CHESHIRE and has been a great fan of ELVIS PRESLEY and THE BEATLES since childhood. *UP ALL NIGHT* and *TAKE ME HOME* are the titles of ONE DIRECTION's albums, and 'LITTLE THINGS' is Harry's favourite song from the second album.

True-fan timeline
Pages 66–69

1. April 2012
2. Justin Bieber
3. 1st February 1994
4. 'Isn't She Lovely'
5. Best British Single
6. Olympics Closing Ceremony

Super-fans
Pages 70–72

1. True Tale	5. True Tale	9. Fan Fake
2. True Tale	6. Fan Fake	10. True Tale
3. Fan Fake	7. True Tale	11. True Tale
4. True Tale	8. True Tale	12. Fan Fake

While it's true that some of these stories appeared in the media, a lot of 'facts' you may read about Harry are just rumours. Keep an open mind, Directioners!

Guess who?
Pages 78–79

1. Shaving off his hair for charity
2. Becoming a lawyer
3. A Harry Styles action figure
4. Harry's hairstylist
5. Zayn Malik
6. Chris Martin of Coldplay

7. Liam Payne
8. The bakery where Harry used to work before he became part of One Direction
9. Taylor Swift

Headline news!
Pages 88–89

'I HAVE 7000 GIRLFRIENDS' – True News

'HARRY STYLES TOO PRETTY TO PLAY FOOTBALL'
– Fake Fail

'HAIRY SPIDER SPIED ON HARRY' – True News

'HARRY STYLES WILL BE UP ALL NIGHT IN SPOOKY NEW HOME' – True News

'I'M A BIG KNIT' – Fake Fail

'HARRY STYLES HANGS OUT WITH JAMES CORDEN. START OF A NEW CELEBRITY BROMANCE?' – True News

'HARRY'S CLOSE ENCOUNTER' – Fake Fail

'HARRY GETS LIPPY' – Fake Fail